ABOUT THIS BOOK

Many children who live in crowded towns and cities seldom get the chance to see farm animals for themselves. This book will serve as an introduction to the wide variety of animals, both domestic and wild, that live on our farms.

The domesticated animals in this book are shown housed in the best conditions to set an example to the child of the sort of care which is expected today.

Children are usually fascinated by animals and their young, and this lively book will help to develop that interest in an entertaining way.

As you read through the book together, encourage the child to question and search the page for interesting details. Simple words have been introduced at the top of the page for the child who is beginning to recognise whole words. If you have visited a farm relate the pictures to the child's experience. If not, try to arrange a farm visit to make the book that much more meaningful.

James Fitzsimmons
(Cert. Ed., Head of Infants)

Rhona Whiteford
(B.A. (Open), Cert. Ed., former Head of Infants)

animals
on the farm

written by
James Fitzsimmons and
Rhona Whiteford

illustrated by Terry Burton

Filmset in Nelson Teaching Alphabet
by kind permission of
Thomas Nelson and Son Ltd.

A CIP catalogue record for this book is available from the British Library.

cattle

Farmers have lots of different kinds of cattle on their farms.

Can you see the black and
white ones?

Cows give us milk.
The farmer milks the cows in the morning and in the evening.

Cheese, cream, butter and yoghurt
are made from milk.
Which is your favourite to eat?

pigs

A mother pig is called a sow.
She has a lot of piglets
at the same time.

How many piglets can you see
in the sty?

turkeys and chickens

Turkeys and chickens walk around
scratching for food on the ground.

Chickens lay eggs.
Do you like eggs for your breakfast?

geese and ducks

Geese and ducks are happiest near
water so that they can swim.

Mother duck teaches her ducklings to
swim as soon as they hatch.

farm cats

Mother cat finds a safe place
to have her kittens.
The barn is warm and dry.

Most cats like meat to eat and milk to drink.

farm dogs

Farmers keep dogs as pets and to help on the farm.

Dogs and puppies love to play.
Have you got a dog as a pet?

sheep

Sheep and their lambs live together in big flocks.

We use sheep's wool to make jumpers.
Do you wear a woolly jumper to
keep warm?

goats

Goats' milk is creamy and very good
to drink.
It also makes good cheese.

The nanny goat's milk helps the kids
to grow big and strong.

horses

Horses love to run and play in the fields.

The little foal looks at the riders.
Have you ever been on a horse?

the farmyard in the morning

The farmyard is a busy place in the morning as everyone sets off for work.

the farmyard at night

At night wild animals come to visit the farmyard in search of food.

Have you looked out of your window
at night time?

in the fields

One day I saw a big brown cow
Raise her head and chew,
I said, "Good morning, Mrs Cow,"
But all she said was, "Moo!"